The
Battle Upstairs

Also by Maci Bookout

Bulletproof

*I Wasn't Born Bulletproof: Lessons I've Learned
(So You Don't Have To)*

*The Maci and Taylor Wedding Album:
An Adult Coloring Book*

The Bottle Upstairs

Poetry Book

New York Times Bestselling Author

MACI BOOKOUT

Post Hill
PRESS

A POST HILL PRESS BOOK
ISBN: 978-1-68261-784-7
ISBN (eBook): 978-1-68261-785-4

The Battle Upstairs:
Poetry Book
© 2020 by Maci Bookout
All Rights Reserved

Cover design and illustrations by Mike Diaz,
    www.MikeDiazTattoo.com
Interior design and layout by Sarah Heneghan,
    sarah-heneghan.com

Post Hill Press
New York • Nashville
posthillpress.com

Published in the United States of America

Table of Contents

It's almost mind blowing,
how much your mind can hold.

—Charlise Turner

This is my room upstairs.
I will show you.

I will not apologize for the
vacancy I create
with my thoughts.

I will not explain the
edits I make
in my attic.

I will not fear the fight
when I face
my battle.

I will not allow anyone else
to write
my story.

I will tell you.
This is my room upstairs.

SHOW AND TELL
———————

Poetry.

It can shatter a brain,

but boy how it can heal a broken heart.

This.

This is why I always come back to it.

LIFEGUARD
_____

We spend so much time
searching for someone
to give our love to,

we forget to give
some of it to ourselves.

SELFLESS

_____

Feeling myself, not feeling
what the world did...
sorry for me.
The world held its breath,
while I provided it.
Shameful place of people,
of what is most beautiful to me.
I fell in love.
Lost what sight I had left
for anything unimportant.
Put pieces of my soul on my structure,
consisting of art too hard to explain.
Permanently shielding me,
giving myself no option to walk away.
Life follows me now,
and I lead the way.

SORRY FOR ME

I want to find myself.
The me that is alone.

The girl I used to know
before she lost her own.

Where's the voice inside my head?
That is the friend I need.

Maybe she ran away,
left the madness to be free.

Did I abandon her
or is she disappointed in me?

Taught myself how to lose control,
now I need to find my peace.

HIDE AND SEEK
_____

Don't ask to walk in

my shoes,

if you're just going to leave

them at the door.

A MILE

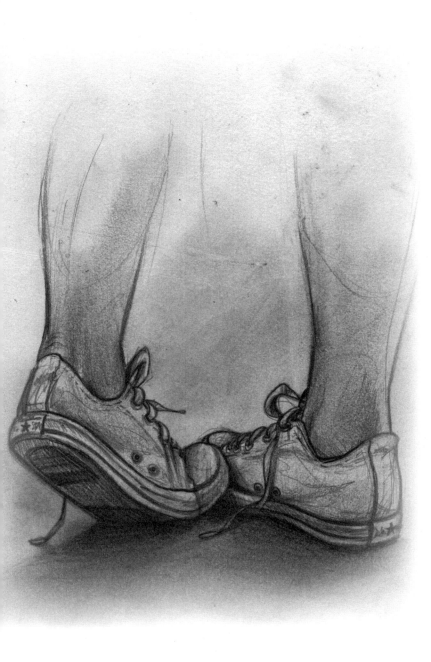

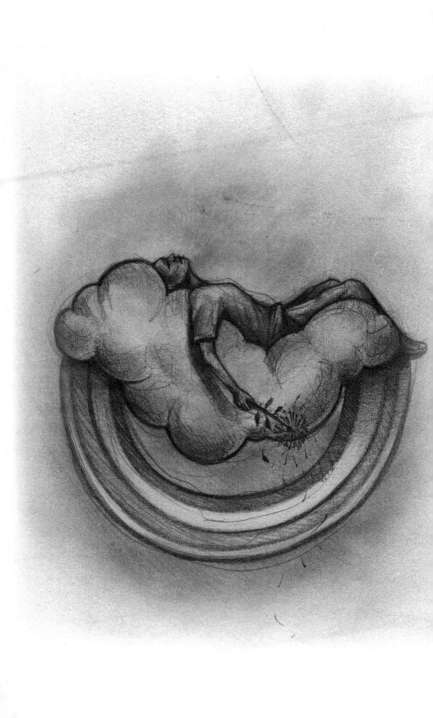

Dark Cloud, why are you so savage?
You stalk the weak and relish in the ravage.
You blur the truth and inspire bondage.
Tell me, how you choose your hostage.

I see the sun slip away seamlessly.
You're drowning the dandelions' dignity.
You derail intuition and bruise the broken.
Take away power as if it's a token.

Dark Cloud, you push the limits.
Camouflage chaos into confetti.
You torture the vein and poison the brain.
You don't care, rich or poor.
You handcuff hostages to a revolving door.

I see the sun slip away seamlessly.
You're drowning the dandelions' dignity.
You derail intuition and bruise the broken.
Take away power as if it's a token.

Dark Cloud, you pretend to have a purpose.
Blunt or bluffing, it's Honey Flavored Stardust.
I can no longer allow you to cover me.
I'll chase the sun back to safety
and pray your hostages cling to recovery.

DARK CLOUD
———

If being alone
makes you feel sad,

it's the perfect time to
learn how to

make yourself happy.

TIME FLIES

Lightning strikes
everyone screams
and goes inside.

A human screams
and everyone goes
on strike,

as if we weren't all created equal.

STRIKES

She was fierce and fearless,
she wasn't simple,
and sometimes she was mad.

She was quiet, and she always had something to say.

She had flaws, and that was okay.

And when she was down,
she got right back up.

She was beautiful, and
she was a beast
in her own way.

She wasn't fragile,
she was unstoppable,
unbreakable.

She liked it that way.

PERFECT

Alone

She stood fearful,

exposed.

Brave in her vulnerability,

humbled.

It was then she could forgive,

her past.

By shedding her armor,

she found herself.

ALONE

She can hear the whispers
even in the silence.

She may have asked for this
but who knew it would be so violent.

In a world with no privacy
she keeps so much quiet.

A handful of thoughts
quickly becomes a riot.

If they knew exactly what she was thinking
would they join her in the silence?

She wonders if she'd still be loved
or be thrown into a crisis.

WONDERWORLD

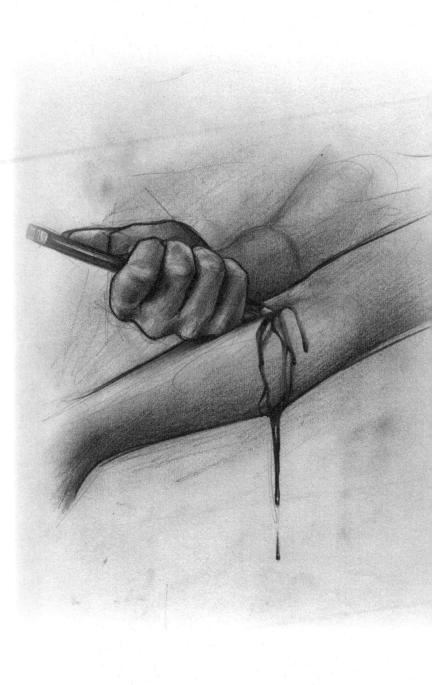

My ink filled veins,
they bleed on paper.

that pencil lead,
came from the bullets fired.

my scars tell a story.

they are markings of where
the fabric of my character was
tested,

but refused to unravel.

TRIED AND TRUE

You live inside your own mind,
there is nothing to unveil.

Your mind is the only thing
you truly own.

Don't let anyone or anything
break you.

Only you can do that.

MIND IF I MATTER

This year has been a test for me,
and through all the times of betrayal
I lost the person I used to be.

I sold her to the people around,
because my efforts were spent on loyalty.
Maybe I let her run away?
I miss the girl I used to be.

Or maybe I forgot to please her
in the midst of all the royalty?
All I have to give is gone.
Is this the payback I'm supposed to see?

But what if I'm not to blame?
I don't know who I'm supposed to be.
Was I meant to fall apart like this?
Because I'm drowning in my own insanity.

BARGAIN

Poetry doesn't rely on comprehension.
Sometimes,
it's sheer interpretation.

PIGGY BANK

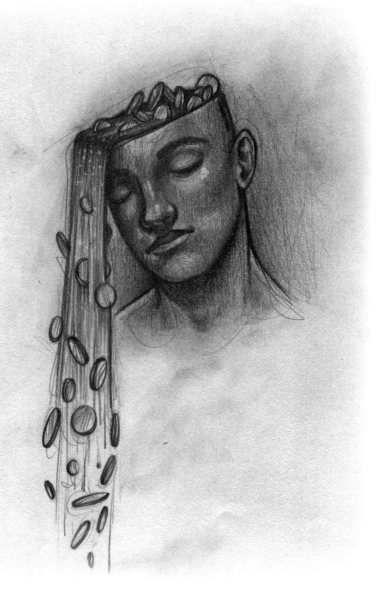

make noise on paper
unable to speak what's felt
no fear in the deck
or the hand that was dealt

back to the bridge
save face all the way
look at the fast life
changing slowly day by day

spade and heart too big
bared by physical being
gutsy rounds of gambles
shuffling and seeing

suits and diamonds either way
have no winner right now
no dealer to judge
the queen questions the vow

place chance on the table
join the club and roll the dice
better hide that chip on your shoulder
don't let the king decide

POKER FACE

Mind, how you wonder.

      Satisfy my wanderlust.

Eyes, when you close,

      adjust the focus to what you chose.

Ears, can you hear

      all the hate thrown around here?

Hands, will you help

      mend the wrongs to write?

Nose, are you there?

      Sense the essence of my soul.

Mouth, when you open,

      keep the flavor of my words tasteful.

UNCOMMON SENSE

That dirty plate
at home,
Clean it up.

To be safe
at home,
again.

Start there
hustle there
miss home.
Walk there
battle there
come home.
Ends there.

There's no place
like home,
safe at home.

SAFE AT HOME
———————

row eighteen
cold blue chair
warmth of a window
sun on her hair
thirty thousand feet
high in the air
inside only questions
of how she arrived there
the flight carries on
life leads the way
perhaps it lasts forever
or ends in a day

ROW EIGHTEEN
———

That white cloud outside the window, you see.

A fixture in the sky, transparency.

Dauntless while hanging in the balance,

cryptic ornament, wavering talents.

Voices share reverence of its purity,

distinct on the side of obscurity.

Ignorant to what the shadow possesses,

voices preaching promises to endure any stresses.

Shady silence underneath the white cloud

abandoned secrets so quickly surround.

How gullible to hold vagabond hands,

trusting promises too selfish to withstand.

Chasing that white cloud outside the window,

beats being stuck under the empty shadow.

SONNET 1: HOW GULLIBLE TO HOLD VAGABOND HANDS

There will come a time
when you've reached a fork in the road.

Take a minute,
pause.

Don't find comfort in that
standstill.

That place is not
your destination.

Navigate the unknown
seek the journey.

Take a look around.
You're not lost as it may seem.

WONDER

Strikethrough or turn the page to refine,

never erase your initial state of mind.

COUPLET: PENCIL

This morning had nothing to hide,
another downpour on its way.

Grab a bottle and hold on tight,
seems to be the usual nowadays.

That bottle drowns the space,
where the pencil used to stay.

Maybe the bottom of the bottle,
the numbness and the taste,

is better than swallowing the words
the pencil lead spit onto the page.

WICKED

Replaying years in my mind
knowing what went wrong.
Remembering that night
aware we weren't that strong.

Letting myself go
allowing ownership to you.
Forgiving struggles created
still something I'd never undo.

Wish it had been known
the pain love could create.
Same question always asked
would I go back and wait.

Sharing time and experience
of what is most beautiful to me.
World full of happy sacrifice
interesting person I came to be.

What is known now
I wouldn't go back and wait.
I'd take the same result
only with someone I don't hate.

GO BACK AND WAIT

Go ahead, tell me things.
Then lie to yourself.
You make wrong okay.
That's fine,
I can rescue myself.

LIE TO YOURSELF

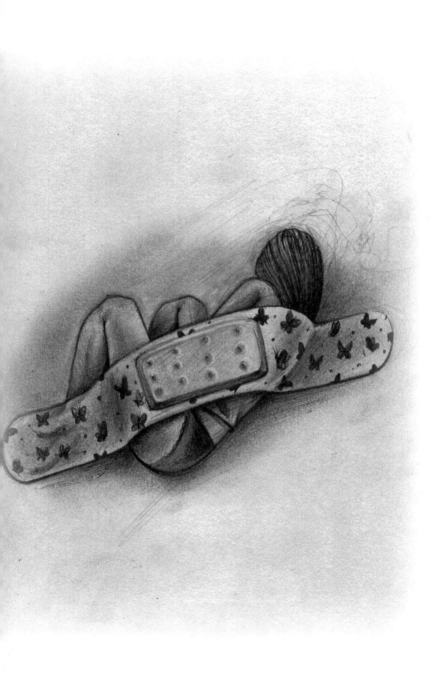

Your lipstick

only looks as good

as the words coming out of your mouth.

PRETTY SHADE

Hope and home,
each so comforting.
How can they be so similar,
yet so confusing?
Standing alone,
they can feel empty.
But together they're
more than satisfying.

HOPE AND HOME

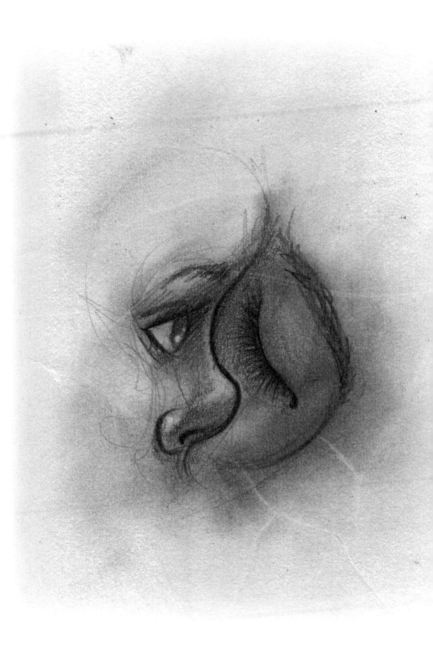

My story started decades ago.
But life as I know it
began when yours did.

A few days away, from a few years.
I'm getting through
what I got myself into.

It's all because of you.
Being beside me
every step of the way.

All I had to offer you was my heart.
From day one,
that's all you ever wanted.

You are my heart.

LOVE YOU MORE

This is a journey of growing up.
Everything I learn I'll teach you,
as you are teaching me.

I'll give you the chance
to have a future
because it's what you gave to me.

If I'm gifted a long life with you,
I promise, as your mother and friend,
I will always love you more.

When I'm gone,
If you learned anything from me,
I hope it's that you love yourself as much as I loved
you.

LOVE YOU MORE
———————

There once was a wild boy named Maverick,
who behaved like a human limerick.
He was spunky and risky,
so being his mom was tricky,
but he was one heck of a sidekick.

LIMERICK: RUGRAT

search in circles
search in depths

like clockwork and shadows
everything has a time and place

the heartwood weak, crumbled
steady crawling with neglect

collect the fragments
embrace the bits and pieces

may the storm pass
leaving the branches to bloom

and rest as a reminder
that the roots are worth
at least a little

Something

HEARTWOOD
_____

Getting lost

     is a great way to find yourself.

LOST AND FOUND

i know i've never been good with words
except when i'm speaking on paper.
so i'll allow the sound to flow
from my pen through ink like vapor.

first i want to thank you
for bringing me back to my comfort zone.
above my notebook, pen in hand
writing my thoughts, being alone.

i'm just sorry it's under these circumstances,
but know what i'm writing to cure.
and no matter how long we are apart
our love will remain pure.

i hope you know what i think of you
and the person that you are.
i'd like to see you grow and learn
while i only watch from afar.

i'll get into what i've been wanting to say
and while you read what i'm speaking,
remember no matter how much i love you
this isn't the pain that you're seeing.

BETTER THAN HERE

i'm not sure where you went,
or why i let you go.
i got tired of fighting for hurt
and i thought i'd let you know.

maybe i'm the one whose running,
not running from what we had
but to where i need to be,
a place without the bad.

i've missed you as my friend.
that's all i want you to be.
maybe by placing you back there
i can learn to be free.

crazy because i'm fine,
but that's all i've ever been.
i want something to feel,
the satisfaction of a win.

please know i care about you,
but i'm so lost on what you mean.
i could never turn my back on you,
i just need to be alone to dream.

BETTER THAN HERE

so while i'm out there facing the world
i want you to do the same,
find out who you really are
so we don't have to play this game.

find yourself and i'll find me
even if it takes forever,
because two lost hearts
will never make it together.

and after we have lived life
as two separate souls,
after we're determined as individuals,
and conquered our separate goals.

then maybe, just maybe
our paths will again cross,
i hope that if they never do
you'll be thankful for this loss.

because my wish for us is to be better apart
even if it takes us years,
even if we never join again
we will both be somewhere better than here.

BETTER THAN HERE

my sleepy mind
such highs, such lows

come inside
where the mess grows

a deep sleep
a place poetry never goes.

SLEEPY

How does distance work?
So close, yet so far,
no plan but to just be.
Listen, it's perfect.
Feeling it empties.

How does love feel?
Selfless and fearless,
warm and exciting.
Listen, it's safe.
Feeling it thrills.

How do hearts beat?
Wounded yet numb,
willing to be scarred.
Listen, it's terrifying.
Feeling it hypnotizes.

How does the story end?
Silence the mind,
steady the heart.
Listen, it's limitless.
Feeling it solidifies.

LISTEN, FEELINGS

Simple thoughts
are complicated
to write down.

DELICATE

Stormy thoughts penned inside,
a blurry bottle not yet dry.

Drifting away from its wreckage,
leaving behind all of the damage.

Struggling to ride the wave that hits,
instead of drowning in it.

High tides roll in, washing ashore,
a stormy message anxious to explore.

Searching for help, but at what cost?
Blurry bottle asks if the storm is lost.

Stormy mumbles, just trying to keep dry,
they both know that's a lie.

Blurry, check the bottle down to the base,
that's where Stormy feels most safe.

.

THIS ONE DESERVES A TITLE

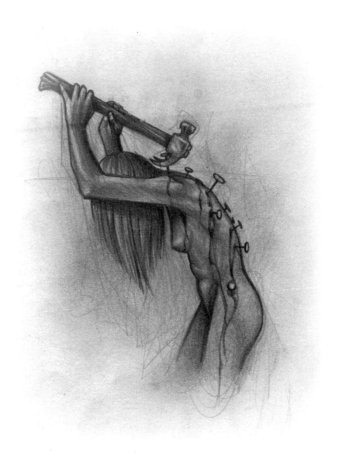

We hand out second chances as if they're limitless,
then we wonder why we can't forgive
ourselves.

EXCUSE

One of those memories,
I'd be smitten by reliving.
I'm being followed by Cupid,
And he's not too forgiving.

Flashbacks of summertime,
I've been living on those.
So maybe Cupid's trail,
Is where my heart goes.

In a southern city,
I've always called home.
That's what you felt like,
Before you were gone.

Irresponsible behavior,
Falling for a stranger.
There was just no time,
To consider the danger.

I wish I knew that night,
What consumed my being.
Warmth I'd forgotten to feel,
Parts of myself I hadn't been seeing.

MAYBE MEMORIES

Fear I'd been running from,
Caught up to my heart.
I never had a choice,
From the very start.

My heart I'd been neglecting,
Damaged and put away.
But you can't help who you love,
I'm scared you're here to stay.

Maybe I'm in love with you,
Even so, I'm not dumb.
You're just like the rest,
So my mind will stay numb.
I've never been here before,
I'll never do this again.
Every bit of my control,
Was gone before you walked in.

Maybe I should shut up,
Maybe you should stay.
Maybe I'm who's running,
Maybe we'll be okay.

MAYBE MEMORIES

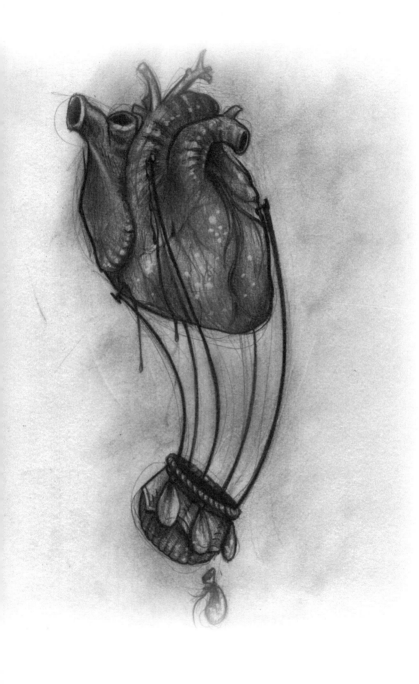

Why do we place
our broken hearts,

back in the bloody hands
that completely tore them apart?

As if the one
so willing to destroy it,

can be trusted to
repair and protect it.

STAINED
_____

I never thought you would come back.
I never waited for you.

So don't be upset
because I am unprepared.

I lost everything about me
when you left.

So forgive me
if that is all I take with me when

I run away this time.

RUNAWAY
———————

Actions you feel,
words you hear.

They say,
actions speak louder than words.

They aren't wrong,
but whoever they are...

Must have never heard
how loud the silence screams,

When you're alone in a room
with a stranger you truly loved.

Silence is the most painful
punch in the gut you'll ever hear.

NOISE
_____

The toughest puzzle.
Beautiful thoughts written down,
then a soul was found.

HAIKU: IRONY

To get her lips on his skin.
Together, peacefully asleep,
peacefully awake.

She adored kissing him.
She felt him, he felt loved.

She admired his tired body,
how he protected her.

He was strong, so was her kiss.

Rush to get her home,
fight to get her kiss.

Love together,
to get her.

TO · GET · HER

Desperate to be clothed
in it,

she had been homesick for his scent.

What once smelled like safety,
now smelled of shame.

It was then she knew

she had escaped.

FREED

Like a thousand-piece puzzle,
messy and scattered,
or just a nasty game of
Would You Rather?

Reference the end result,
fight to make it better.
Heart arguing the brain
just to put the pieces together.

Can you build it back?
Better than it was before?
Or will your mind give up
hoping for something more?

HYPOCRITE

I write about things
I'm too afraid to feel.

I speak about things
people are too afraid to face.

I act in a way I believe is right,
ignoring those who want me to be wrong.

I care about what people think of themselves,
rather than what is thought of me.

I have experiences that nobody knows,
through them all I have loved myself.

I know who I was born to be,
a mother who wanted to make a difference.

So I did.

PICTURE FRAME

Poetry can become something more
to the person that wrote it...
after hearing what it means
to the person that read it.

END PAGE

They all stared at me.

Eyes watching, some
Judging, some thinking,
"We know what you've done"
As if it was a secret.

I carry my naivety, my
Carelessness, my bad decision
On my body, with a dignity and a pride
That I don't feel, but have to show.

Some pretend to sympathise,
To care but I don't need it.
What I did is what is and
I'm happy.

Still

Every time they see me
They are reminded of my sins
By the big round
Bump.

I AM BULLETPROOF

Beautiful on some, it is
A mark of femininity but somehow
On me it is a
Mark of shame

I refuse to care or feel
The sorrow and disgust of my neighbours.
What I did is what is and
I'm happy.

I'll survive. I'll even thrive
And prove these people wrong.
All on my own.

I'm bulletproof.

—Anonymous

I AM BULLETPROOF

About the Poet

Maci Bookout starred on the MTV reality TV show *16 and Pregnant* and went on to become a fan favorite on the spin-off *Teen Mom*. Known for her down-to-earth Southern charm and level-headed personality, Maci has earned the respect of teens and adults alike with her courage under pressure and her mature reflections on teen pregnancy and motherhood. Maci has appeared on numerous talk shows and spoken to many educational groups on teen pregnancy prevention. She consistently receives praise from the audience for her candidness, down to earth personality, and refreshingly insightful commentary. Maci also makes personal appearances at marketing/promotional events, keynote speeches, colleges, TV shows, sporting events, and other unique spokesperson/appearance opportunities. In addition to being a public speaker, writer, and TV/radio host, Maci is a mom to three children and married to Taylor McKinney.